My Little House in the Big Woods

Homeschool Workbook

By Kimberly M. Hartfield, B.S., M.S.

Table of Contents

Laura and Almanzo Wilder	p. 3
Introduction	p. 4
Chapter 1	p. 5
Chapter 2	p. 6
Chapter 3	p. 7
Chapter 4	p. 8
Chapter 5	p. 9
Chapter 6	p.10
Chapter 7/8	p.11
Chapter 9	p.12
Chapter 10	p.13
Chapter 11	p.14
Chapter 12	p.15
Chapter 13	p.16
Draw Your Pictures	p.17-19
Chapter Answers	p.20-23
Laura Ingalls Wilder Biography	p.24

Laura and Almanzo Wilder 1885

Introduction

One of my fondest memories is reading the Little House books to my girls and boys for the first time. I hadn't read them myself till I was grown and had my first child, while sitting in a rocking chair nursing my baby. But when they were old enough I knew I had to read those wonderful stories of a time gone by to let them experience it for themselves. The kids loved Laura's stories as much as I did, and together we discovered a world that we never knew, but wish we had.

When I began homeschooling the last two of my eight children, the Little House books were the first on our reading list. I created these worksheets to go along with our reading and found them very helpful to us as homeschoolers. I put them up on my website and they got more views than I had ever imagined. So I knew there was a need for them and I had hoped to make them available at little or no cost to homeschoolers, as I know how expensive homeschool materials can cost.

I believe these will be even more useful in a printed booklet, so I decided to publish them in a more traditional method, in a workbook format. I hope this workbook will help parents and children learn together and encourage them to learn about some of the old ways of doing things. I hope that users will find them a great help in their homeschool endeavors.

Little House in the Big Woods

Chapter 1

1. Who is the author of Little House in the Big Woods?

2. In what state did the story take place?

3. Who were the main characters in the story?

4. Why was Laura sometimes afraid to go to sleep at night?

5. What was Laura's dog's name?

6. What did Pa do to preserve their meat for the winter?

7. Name two things Jack did to help the family?

8. What was used to make a balloon for Laura and Mary?

9. What was Laura's doll, Susan, made of?

10. What instrument did Pa play in the evenings?

Activities: Choose 1 or 2

- Look up Laura Ingalls Wilder in an encyclopedia.
- Look up Wisconsin on the Internet.
- Draw a picture of a wolf, dog, or cat and color.
- Try some beef or venison jerky.
- Make a corncob doll
- Have a visitor play a fiddle.
- Plant a garden in a cup (onions, carrots, lettuce, radishes)

Little House in the Big Woods

Chapter 2 Winter Days and Winter Nights

1. What did Pa do in the winter to have meat for the family?

2. What chores did Laura and Mary have?

3. Ma used to say,

    Wash on Monday
    Iron on Tuesday
    Mend on Wednesday
    Churn on Thursday
    Clean on Friday
    Bake on Saturday
    _____ on Sunday

4. What did Ma use to color the butter they churned in winter?

5. What did Ma make for Laura and Mary to play with?

6. What did Pa call Laura for fun?

7. What game did Pa play with Laura and Mary that scared them?

8. What song did Pa sing?

9. What was in the bottom of the glass bowl of the kerosene lamp that kept it from exploding?

10. What story did Pa tell Laura and Mary?

Activities: Choose 1 or 2

- Make a chore chart for daily and weekly chores
- Make paper dolls out of magazines and cardstock
- Talk about the difference between nicknames and name calling that is hurtful
- Sing Yankee Doodle
- Look up panthers in encyclopedia or draw picture and color

Little House in the Big Woods

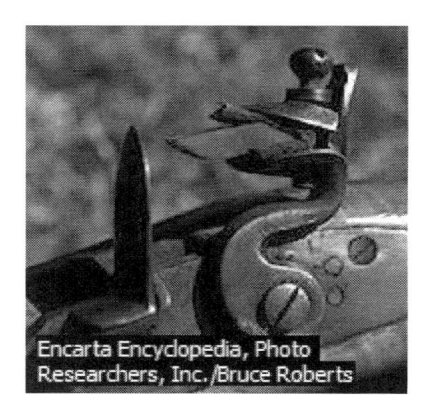

Chapter 3 The Long Rifle

1. What did Pa keep on the hooks over the door?

2. What did Pa make for his gun?

3. Why did Laura burn her fingers?

4. What was Pa's bullet pouch made of?

5. What new story did Pa tell the girls?

6. What was Pa supposed to be doing when he was playing in the woods?

7. What asked Pa "Who"?

8. Where were the cows?

9. What did Pa's father whip him with?

10. Why did Pa's father whip him?

Activities: Choose 1 or 2

- Talk about being responsible and obedient
- Talk about why a parent might discipline a child
- Talk about gun safety or have a qualified visitor
- Look up owls or draw a picture and color.

Little House in the Big Woods

Chapter 4 Christmas

1. What did Pa make Ma for Christmas?

2. What did Ma put on the shelf that Pa made her?

3. What did Laura and Mary pour on the snow?

4. Who came to visit Laura's family?

5. What did Laura and Mary play with the cousins?

6. What did Prince, the dog, protect Aunt Eliza from?

7. What did all the children find in their stockings on Christmas morning?

8. What special gift did Laura get for Christmas?

9. What did Laura name her doll?

10. What did Santa put in the stockings of Naughty children?

11. What two books did the children look at pictures in?

12. What did Ma give the cousins to put in their pockets to keep their fingers warm?

Activities: Choose 1 or 2

- Talk about making homemade Christmas presents. Ask what the kids could make for their family members?
- Look up panthers or draw a picture and color
- Make Christmas stockings out of construction paper
- Make a rag doll with a parent's help
- Look up Christmas and find out the true origin of Santa Claus, Watch a Veggie Tales Movie about Christmas, Read the Christmas story from the Bible

Little House in the Big Woods

Chapter 5 Sundays

1. What did Laura and Mary do on Sundays?

2. What was the name of Pa's big green book?

3. What was Laura's favorite picture in the Bible?

4. What story did Pa tell Laura about Sundays?

5. What did Grandpa and his brothers do when their father fell asleep?

6. What did the boys run into on the road?

7. What happened to the boys when Sunday was over?

8. What did Pa give Laura for her birthday to keep her doll, Charlotte, company?

9. What else did Laura get for her birthday?

10. What song did Pa play for Laura's birthday?

Activities: Choose 1 or 2

- Draw and color a picture of Adam naming the animals
- Discuss what your family does on Sundays
- Talk about birthdays and have a party
- Sing "Pop, Goes the Weasel"
- Read or memorize Genesis 2:19-20 about Adam naming the animals

Little House in the Big Woods

Chapter 6 Two Big Bears

1. Why did Pa go to town in the spring?

2. Why didn't Pa take his gun to town with him?

3. Why had Laura and Mary never seen a town?

4. What kind of lantern did Laura carry for Ma to milk the cow?

5. What was standing at the barnyard gate?

6. What might have happened if Laura had not immediately done what her mother told her to do?

7. What did Pa bring from town for Laura and Mary?

8. What colors were Laura and Mary's dresses?

9. What story did Pa tell the girls when he came home?

10. What was the bear in the way?

11. What was the prayer Laura and Mary said every night?

12. Why didn't Pa build the fire back up?

Activities: Choose 1 or 2

- Look up bears or spring or draw a picture and color
- Learn the prayer
- Talk about obedience and why it is so important to do what your told immediately
- Make a tin lantern- Fill a tin can with water and freeze. When completely frozen, hammer nail holes in a pretty pattern on the sides of the can. Make two nail holes near the top of the can on opposite sides. Put a piece of wire through them to make a handle. Put a votive candle inside when the ice melts enough to remove it.

Little House in the Big Woods

Chapter 7/8 The Sugar Snow and Dance at Grandpa's

1. What was the sugar snow?

2. What did Pa bring back from Grandpa's house?

3. What did grandpa make the buckets out of?

4. Why did he use those woods to make the buckets?

5. What is hasty pudding made of?

6. What is a yoke?

7. Why was Uncle George "wild"?

8. What are corsets and petticoats?

9. What kind of dance did everyone do?

10. What kind of dance did Grandma and Uncle George do?

Activities: Choose 1 or 2

- Talk about war and why that might affect people negatively
- Look up dancing, and learn about square dancing or a jig.
- Look up maple syrup and learn how it is made
- Research bucket making
- Make hasty pudding and eat it for breakfast with maple syrup
- Make a yoke out of a sturdy oak stick with a parents help
- Research clothing from the past

Little House in the Big Woods

Going to Town Chapter 9

1. Name some of the wild flowers in the woods around Laura's home.

2. From what did Pa make Laura's swing?

3. What kind of animals did they keep on the farm?

4. Why didn't they eat fresh meat in the spring and summer?

5. How far was it from Laura's house to the town?

6. What was the name of the town Laura's family visited?

7. How were the houses in town different from Laura's house?

8. What are some of the things Laura saw in the store?

9. What kind of candy did the girls get?

10. Why did Laura's pocket tear out of her dress?

11. What lesson do you think she learned from this?

Activities: Choose 1 or 2

- Talk about being greedy verses being unselfish
- Look up wildflowers in your state and learn their names
- Make a swing with a parent
- Look up farm animals and learn how to care for them
- Look up farming or go visit a local farm

Little House in the Big Woods

Chapter 10 Summer Time

1. What country was Mrs. Peterson from?

2. How could you divide two cookies fairly between 3 people?

3. What was Laura's cat's name?

4. Why did Laura slap Mary's face? Was it right for her to do so?

5. Why didn't Pa play the fiddle much in the summer?

6. What chores did Laura and Mary do in the summer?

7. Why did a calf have to be killed to make cheese?

8. What is green cheese?

9. What did Pa find in the woods?

10. Why didn't the bear attack Pa?

Activities: Choose 1or 2

- Look up Sweden on the Internet or in an encyclopedia
- Look up cats or draw a picture and color it.
- Look up and learn about how cheese is made today
- Look up and learn about bee keeping and making honey today
- Plant a garden in a cup or transplant previously grown plants to the garden

Little House in the Big Woods

Chapter 11 Harvest

1. What is a cradle?

2. How was a shock of wheat made?

3. Why did the grain have to be in a shock before nightfall?

4. Why did the oats have to be cut and shocked before the winter rains came?

5. How old was Pa when he had to do a good day's work?

6. What did Charlie do when he went to the field to work with Pa and Uncle Henry?

7. Why do you think Uncle Henry didn't whip Charlie?

8. What was the result of Charlie's behavior?

9. What do ma and Aunt Polly do to help Charlie?

10. How can someone be a liar without saying a word?

Activities: Choose 1or 2

- Look up and learn about growing oats today
- Look up and learn about yellow jackets and other bees and wasps.
- Talk about responsibility, obedience, and natural consequences and punishment
- Look up and learn about home remedies and medicinal herbs
- Talk about being truthful in words and actions

Little House in the Big Woods

Chapter 12 The Wonderful Machine

1. What did Ma do with the oat straw?

2. What kind of nuts did Laura, Mary, and Ma gather?

3. How did they preserve the nuts?

4. What chores did Laura and Mary do in the Fall?

5. What are some of the things they ate?

6. What was the wonderful machine used for?

7. What was Johnny Cake and why was it called that?

8. Why did they use the machine to thresh the wheat?

9. What were the two parts of the machine called?

10. Why was the machine called an eight horsepower machine?

Activities: Choose 1 or 2

- Look up and learn about straw hat making.
- Draw a picture related to Harvest Time and color
- Talk about Thanksgiving and Harvest time
- Look up and learn about growing wheat today
- Look up nuts and learn about different kinds
- Look up and learn about early machines used for harvesting and compare to modern machines used for harvesting today
- Look up and learn about the Civil War

Little House in the Big Woods

Chapter 13 The Deer in the Wood

1. What did Laura and Mary make when it turned cold?

2. What was a deer-lick?

3. Why did Pa make a deer-lick?

4. What did Pa do to the house to help it stay warm in the winter?

5. Why do you think Pa didn't shoot the bear or deer?

6. What songs did Pa play on his fiddle?

7. What does *Auld Lang Syne* mean?

8. What is your favorite part of Little House in the Big Woods? Write a paragraph or two about it? Older Children may write 1-3 page book report.

Activities: Choose 1or 2

- Get someone to teach you how to knit
- Make a small nine-patch quilt potholder. Younger children can make a patchwork out of construction paper and glue.
- Talk about how families got their food in the past as compared to how they get their food now.
- Sing Auld Lang Syne or Oh Susana
- Talk about hunting safety and or animal conservation

Draw your pictures here.

Draw your pictures here.

Draw your pictures here.

Chapter Answers

Chapter 1 Answers

1. Laura Ingalls Wilder
2. Wisconsin
3. Laura, Mary, Pa, Ma, Baby Carrie
4. The wolves
5. Jack
6. He smoked and salted it.
7. He kept the wolves out and chased the deer out of the garden.
8. A pig's bladder
9. A corncob
10. A fiddle

Chapter 2 Answers

1. Trapped animals
2. wiped the dishes and made the bed
3. rest
4. carrot juice
5. paper dolls
6. half-pint
7. mad dog
8. Yankee Doodle
9. salt
10. Grandpa and the Panther

Chapter 3 Answers

1. His gun
2. the bullets
3. because she touched the hot bullets
4. buckskin
5. Pa and the Voice in the Woods
6. Bringing home the cows
7. a screech owl
8. the cows were beside the barn
9. a switch
10. to remind him to be obedient

Chapter 4 Answers

1. A wooden shelf
2. The china doll
3. Syrup, candy
4. Aunt Eliza, Uncle Peter, Peter, Alice, Ella, (Aunt, Uncle, cousins)
5. Making snow pictures
6. A panther
7. Red mittens and peppermint candy
8. A rag doll
9. Charlotte
10. Switches
11. Pa's big green book and the Bible
12. A baked potato

Chapter 5 Answers

1. Looked at their paper dolls and listened to Ma read Bible stories or stories from Pa's big green book
2. The Wonders of the Animal world
3. Adam naming the animals
4. Grandpa's Sled and the Pig
5. Went sledding down the hill
6. a pig, hog
7. They got a whipping
8. a little wooden man
9. a new dress for Charlotte and five little cakes
10. Pop, Goes the Weasel

Chapter 6 Answers

1. to trade furs
2. There were too many furs to carry
3. because the nearest town was far away
4. A tin lantern with a candle inside
5. a bear
6. Answers will vary
7. calico for dresses and candy
8. Laura had a red calico and Mary had a blue calico
9. Pa and the Bear in the Way
10. a stump that was burned black
11. *Now I lay me down to sleep*
    I pray the Lord My soul to keep
    If I should die before I wake
    I pray the Lord my soul to take

12. Spring was coming

21

Chapter 7/8 Answers

1. When it snowed again after a warm spell in spring, more sugar could be made.
2. Two cakes of brown Maple sugar and a bucket of Maple syrup.
3. Cedar and white ash
4. Because it wouldn't give a bad taste to the syrup.
5. Yellow corn meal, boiling salted water, served with maple syrup
6. A wooden bar cut to fit around the neck and shoulders to help carry heavy things.
7. because he had run away to be a drummer boy in the army
8. Ladies underclothes from the past
9. A square dance
10. A jig

Chapter 9 Answers

1. Buttercups, violets, thimble flowers, star flowers
2. A piece of tough bark
3. Cows, pigs, chickens
4. To give the baby animals time to grow up
5. 7 miles
6. Pepin
7. They were boarded houses and were built close together
8. Calico cloth, kegs of nails, gunshot, pails of candy, tea, salt, sugar, a plowshare, ax heads, hammer heads, saws, knives, shoes, boots, etc.
9. Valentine hearts
10. Because she put too many pebbles in it
11. Answers will vary. (not to be so greedy)

Chapter 10 Answers

1. Sweden
2. Divide them in thirds and each person gets 2/3 of a cookie
3. Black Susan
4. Because Mary was being prideful and Laura was jealous. No, it's never right to hit someone even if you think you have good reason.
5. Summer days were longer and he was tired after working the fields.
6. Weed the garden, feed the animals, gather the eggs, and help their mother.
7. To get rennet, the lining of a very young calf's stomach
8. Unripened, new cheese
9. A bee tree
10. It was fat and full of honey.

Chapter 11 Answers

1. A sharp steel blade with a wooden framework used for cutting and holding stalks of grain.
2. They stood five bundles upright with the oat heads up and put two on top to make a roof to shelter the grain from rains.
3. It would spoil if it laid on the dewy ground all night
4. They would lose the crop and the horses would be hungry all winter.
5. 11 years old
6. He hid the whetstone, didn't bring the water jug when called, got in the way, and screamed like something was wrong when nothing was.
7. He spoiled him. Answers may vary.
8. He jumped up and down on a yellow jackets' nest and got severely stung.
9. They plastered him with mud and wrapped him in a sheet. They gave him a medicinal herb drink for fever.
10. Your actions can lie as well as your words. Answers may vary.

Chapter 12 Answers

1. She made new hats for the family.
2. walnuts, hickory nuts, and hazel nuts
3. The dried them in the sun and beat the outer hulls off of them.
4. They gathered nuts and harvested the vegetables in the garden.
5. Cabbage and beans, hulled corn and milk, dried berry pies, stewed pumpkin and bead, baked squash with butter.
6. To thresh the wheat (separate the grain from the stalks).
7. It was cornbread. Southern soldiers were called Jonnie Rebs and ate a lot of it.
8. They used it to save time and get more grain off the stalks.
9. The separator and the horsepower
10. Because it used eight horses to work it.

Chapter 13 Answers

1. Patchwork quilts
2. A place where deer came to get salt that was poured out on the ground.
3. To attract the deer to an area he was hunting
4. He banked it with dead leaves and straw and held it all down with stones.
5. Because they were so beautiful he forgot to shoot them.
6. Oh Susana, Auld Lang Syne
7. The days of a long time ago
8. Answers will vary

Laura Ingalls Wilder

Laura Ingalls Wilder (1867-1957) was an American writer, famous for a series of books for children known together as the Little House books. Laura was born near Pepin, Wisconsin. She was homeschooled in the first years of her education and later went to a public school to train to be a teacher. She taught for several years before marrying a farmer, Almanzo Wilder, in 1885. She had her daughter, Rose, shortly after her marriage and a son, who died shortly after birth. After enduring many hardships in the early years of their marriage, Laura and Almanzo moved to Mansfield, Missouri in 1894 and settled on Rocky Ridge Farm.

When Wilder was in her sixties, her daughter, Rose, compelled her to write down her memories of her childhood growing up on the American frontier. The Little House series, based on Laura's life, gives a realistic portrayal of pioneer life, full of warmth, wisdom, humor, and drama. Beginning with *Little House in the Big Woods* (1932), in the Wisconsin cabin where she was born, Wilder records her family's westward movement to the *Little House on the Prairie* (1935) in Kansas, to Minnesota *On the Banks of Plum Creek* (1937), and lastly to the Dakota Territory in *By the Shores of Silver Lake* (1939). *The Long Winter* (1940), *Little Town on the Prairie* (1941), and *These Happy Golden Years* (1943) describe Laura's teenage years, her first teaching positions, and her marriage to Almanzo Wilder, whose childhood story is told in *Farmer Boy* (1933), which is included in the series.

Three books were published after Laura's death: *The First Four Years* (1971), the last in the Little House series, which tells of Laura and Almanzo's early married life; *On the Way Home*: The Diary of a Trip from South Dakota to Mansfield, Missouri, in 1894, with her daughter, Rose Wilder Lane (1962); and *West from Home* (1974), a collection of letters she wrote to Almanzo while visiting San Francisco in 1915. Roger Lea MacBride, editor of *West From Home* and Lane's adopted grandson, has written two books which continue the Wilders' story and which are told from Rose's perspective; *Little House on Rocky Ridge* (1993) and *Little Farm in the Ozarks* (1994). There are also books from the Caroline years, as well. *Little House in Brookfield* and *Little Town at the Crossroads* were written by Maria D. Wilkes, which covers Laura's mother, Caroline's early years.

Starting with *On the Banks of Plum Creek*, the last five Little House books published during Laura's lifetime were named Newbery Honor Books. In 1954 she received the first Laura Ingalls Wilder Award, given by the American Library Association. Named in her honor, this award is presented every three years to an author or illustrator who has made a "substantial and lasting contribution" to literature for children. Laura's Little House books were the inspiration for one of the most popular television series, "Little House on the Prairie," produced by Michael Landon, who starred as Pa. The TV series, loosely based on Laura's books, aired in the 1970s and 1980s and still shows as re-runs today.

Microsoft ® Encarta ® Reference Library 2005. © 1993-2004 Microsoft Corporation. All rights reserved.

Other books by Kimberly M. Hartfield

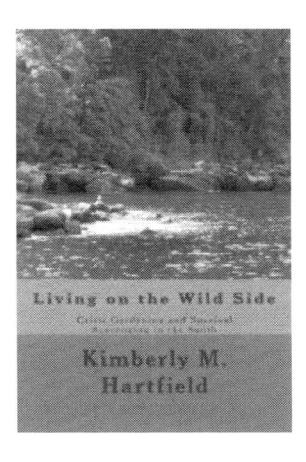

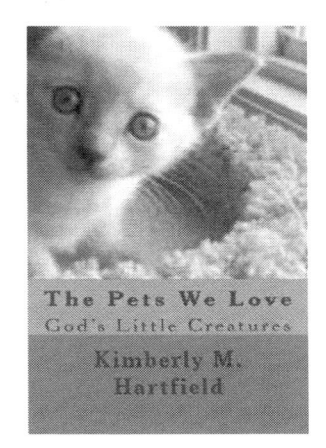

Living on the Wild Side *The Pets We Love*

A Little Redneck Theology   *Don't be Silent: Stop Domestic Violence*   *Silent Screams: on Sexual Violence*

available at
http://gofishministries.wordpress.com

and on Amazon

Made in United States
Troutdale, OR
09/27/2023